STARS OF SPORT

JAROMIR JAGR

BY RAYMOND H. MILLER

j
796.962
Jagr, J
MIL

KH
KIDHAVEN
PRESS™

THOMSON
GALE

San Diego • Detroit • New York • San Francisco • Cleveland
New Haven, Conn. • Waterville, Maine • London • Munich

LIBRARY OF CONGRESS CATALOGING-IN-PUBLICATION DATA

Miller, Raymond H., 1967–
  Jaromir Jagr / by Raymond H. Miller.
  p. cm. — (Stars of sport)
Summary: A biography of the Czechoslovakian-born hockey player whose break-away speed and superb passing and shooting skills have made him one of the premier players in the NHL.
Includes bibliographical references and index.
  ISBN 0-7377-1539-1 (hardback : alk. paper)
1. Jagr, Jaromir, 1972—Juvenile literature   2. Pittsburgh Penguins (Hockey team)—Biography—Juvenile literature.   3. Hockey players—Czech Republic—Biography—Juvenile literature. [1. Jagr, Jaromir, 1972– 2. Hockey players.]
I. Title. II. Series.
  GV844 .5.J35M55 2003
  796.962'092—dc21

2002156051

Contents

Impact Player

J aromir Jagr is considered to be one of the greatest hockey players in the world. His combination of size, strength, and speed is unrivaled in the National Hockey League (NHL). And his electrifying skills on the ice allow him to make an impact on each game in which he plays.

But Jagr's rise to the top was not easy. He was raised in a Communist society in which the government controlled many aspects of people's lives, such as where they worked, how much money they were paid, and where they could travel. Jagr hated living under those conditions, and hockey became his escape. He started playing at age three and quickly advanced through the various age levels, often competing against older boys. He worked hard and his family made sacrifices to make sure he would become a great player. When he could not afford a weight set, his father made him a set of homemade barbells. He also took hundreds of shots at a homemade goal set up in his yard after working on a farm most of the day. The extra practice made him an excellent shooter on the ice.

Born and raised in Czechoslovakia, Jaromir Jagr overcame many obstacles to become one of the greatest hockey players in the world.

His hard work paid off. In 1989, at the age of seventeen, Jagr was talented enough to join Czechoslovakia's national team. A short time later he was drafted by the Pittsburgh Penguins. This team won hockey's top prize, the **Stanley Cup**, in each of his first two seasons.

Despite the Penguins' success, Jagr struggled to find his place on the team and in a new country. He suffered through a long scoring slump and became extremely homesick. He eventually turned things around, and by age nineteen was an **all-star**. Jagr later won the NHL scoring title five times. He received hockey's highest individual honor when he was named Most Valuable Player (MVP) of the league in 1999.

Today Jagr is playing for a new team, the Washington Capitals. He ranks among the fifty leading scorers of all time and is certain to move up the list as he continues his career. But individual awards are not as important to Jagr as they once were. Instead his goal is to win another Stanley Cup championship and make the people of his homeland proud.

CHAPTER
ONE

Breaking
Free

J aromir Jagr was born on February 15, 1972, in
Kladno, Czechoslovakia (now called the Czech
Republic), which is not far from the capital city of
Prague. He lived in Kladno with his parents, Jaromir and
Anna Jagr, and his older sister, Jitka. Long before Jaromir
was born, life was a struggle for the Jagr family. In 1948
the Communist Party took complete control of the
Czechoslovakian government. They seized Jaromir's
grandparents' farmland and three-quarters of their live-
stock. When the government ordered his grandfather,
who was also named Jaromir Jagr, to work at his own
farm for free, he refused and was put in jail. He was re-
leased two years later, but was jailed again in 1968 just
before the Prague Spring, a revolt by the Czech people

against the Communist government. This revolt was later stopped forcefully when troops from the Soviet Union and several other Communist nations invaded Czechoslovakia.

When Jaromir was a boy, life in Czechoslovakia was not any easier. His father and mother both worked long hours to make enough money for the family, and he spent much of his time with his grandmother, Jarmila Jagr. She lived with Jaromir and his parents and sister. "My parents worked the farm and at the factory," he recalls. "I was raised by my grandmother who told me about my grandfather. . . . He died in prison as a political prisoner in the first year of occupation—in '68."[1]

Jaromir's grandmother had a lot of influence on him. Over time he grew to share her dislike of the Communist government. He considered his grandfather a hero, and admired the brave Czech people who stood up to the Soviet Union during the 1968 uprising.

Natural Skater

Through the years, sports had created a close bond among the Czech people. Playing or watching sports often took

Soviet troops march through Prague in 1968. Jaromir disliked the Communist government for making life so difficult for his grandparents.

their minds off the hard times. Ice hockey was the nation's most popular sport, and many boys and men played either leisurely or competitively. The Jagrs were no different. Jaromir's father had been a promising player in his youth. But his dreams of a professional career ended when he injured his knee. He was eager to teach his son the sport.

When Jaromir was three years old his father took him to a frozen pond close to home and taught him how to skate. Jaromir was a natural. He showed great balance on his skates and was soon speeding around the ice swinging his hockey stick at the puck.

On the weekends, Jaromir's mother took him to a local skating rink to practice. He became such a good skater that the figure skating coaches at the rink tried to talk him into signing up for lessons. Jaromir declined because he was becoming more interested in hockey.

Jaromir started playing competitively a year later when his father signed him up for a beginner's hockey league at Pracovni Zalohy (PZ) Kladno, a local sports club. He made a good impression on the coaches. His early start on the ice had made him an excellent skater, and he could handle the puck better than most of the players his age.

Shy Boy

One more year at the beginner's level was all Jaromir needed before he advanced. His father then signed the six-year-old up to play in three separate age levels. One of the levels was for ten-year-olds. This proved to be a challenge. "When I played against other six-year-olds, I

Jagr tries to drive the puck past a defender. The hockey star began to develop his skills at the age of six.

was great," Jaromir Jagr says. "When I played against 10-year-olds, I was average. [My father] wanted me to play where I was average."[2]

Jaromir's father hoped his son would rise to the level of his older competition. That eventually happened, but the experience did have a negative effect. The older players on the team had formed a close bond with one another and did not want someone as young as Jaromir hanging around them after practice. With few companions on the team Jaromir spent much of his time alone and became very shy.

By the time Jagr was eight years old, he was spending a lot of time on the ice practicing by himself. He had no friends on the team his own age.

Jaromir spent more time on the ice to take his mind off the loneliness. At age eight he practiced up to four hours a day during the week and played in three or four games on the weekends. After school he played street hockey with his father in the dirt yard between the house and barn. His blazing **slap shots** smacked the side of the barn, scattering the chickens his mother kept in the yard.

Reagan Admirer

Although Jaromir was a good student in the classroom, he did not always listen to his teachers. "In school we were always taught the Soviet doctrine," he says. "The U.S.A. was bad and wanted war. Russia was our friend and was preventing the United States from bombing us. Even my father didn't tell me the truth, because he was afraid I'd say something in school that would get us into trouble."[3]

But Jaromir knew the Soviet Union was the real enemy from the stories his grandmother had told him. He soon began displaying some of his grandfather's rebellious ways. He secretly admired U.S. president Ronald Reagan, who had called the Soviet Union an "evil empire."[4] Jaromir cut out a photo of Reagan from a magazine and boldly carried it in his textbook to class. One day his teacher found the photo when she picked up his book to write down a test score. She scolded him and told him never to bring the Reagan photo to school again. But he did not listen. Jaromir returned to class each day with the photo tucked in his book.

As Jaromir got older he realized he did not want his entire life to be controlled by the government. He loved his family and his country, but he dreamed of someday living freely in the United States—and playing hockey in the NHL.

CHAPTER Two

The Kladno Kid

At age ten Jaromir started competing in tournaments for PZ Kladno against some of the best Czech players in his age group. Many of the boys he faced were stronger, faster, and had better skills than he did. This made him realize that to become the best, he had to work harder than those players. So that is what he decided to do.

Every day in the summer Jaromir jogged to the family farm, located five miles from his home. He fed the animals and brought in the hay. This made his arms stronger. He did not mind the hard work because the money he earned was used to buy better skates. When the work was done he did not rest. He jogged back home and practiced hockey—hitting up to six hundred slap shots at a homemade goal his father set up in the yard.

Jaromir also lifted weights to gain strength on the ice. But in Czechoslovakia material items such as weights were considered a luxury. So Jaromir's father made a set of barbells out of a spare tractor axle and some metal plates. An old trunk covered with towels served as a

Jagr (center) scrambles for the puck. Throughout his childhood, Jagr trained hard, and he gained enough skill to compete against the best players in Czechoslovakia.

weight bench. Jaromir bench-pressed the weights to gain upper-body strength. And hundreds of deep knee bends with the weights gave him a powerful lower body.

Jaromir's hard work paid off. By the time he was a teenager he had gained enough strength and speed to compete with the best players in Czechoslovakia. His shooting and puck-handling skills were also much improved.

Hockey Hero

In 1985, when Jaromir was thirteen years old, he watched the International Ice Hockey Federation (IIHF) World Championships—a tournament held each year to determine which nation has the best hockey team in the world. That year the games were played in Czechoslovakia's capital city of Prague, and Jaromir was thrilled that the best amateur hockey players in the game were competing in a tournament so close to his home. He watched the games with great interest and cheered for his beloved Czech men's national team.

As the tournament unfolded, a tall and extremely gifted player from Canada caught Jaromir's attention. He was nineteen-year-old Mario Lemieux, a player many hockey experts compared to the sport's greatest star, Wayne Gretzky. Jaromir was amazed at the Canadian's incredible puck-handling and skating skills. He watched Lemieux gracefully maneuver around the ice helping his teammates score **goals** with his accurate passing ability.

Lemieux quickly became Jaromir's favorite player when the Canadian led his team to a 3-1 victory over Czecho-

Mario Lemieux holds the Stanley Cup over his head in 1991. Lemieux was Jagr's favorite hockey player when Jagr was a teenager.

slovakia's rival, the powerful Soviet Union. After the tournament, Jaromir hung a poster of Lemieux on his bedroom wall and often looked at it for inspiration. On the ice he copied the Canadian's shooting and passing skills, while attempting to skate with the same effortless style.

Lemieux was the first pick in the 1984 NHL draft. He was selected by the Pittsburgh Penguins, who became Jaromir's favorite team.

Teen Sensation

Jaromir rapidly climbed the hockey ranks. In 1986 he made the Poldi Kladno junior team—one level below pro. There he scored a remarkable thirty-five goals and thirty-five **assists** in just thirty games. Two years later he was invited to play for the Poldi Kladno professional team. Members of this team played in the best hockey league in Czechoslovakia.

Joining the pros at age fifteen was a remarkable feat, because most of the players in the league were much older than that. Jagr thought he was prepared for the high level of competition, because he had grown up playing—and succeeding—against older boys. But he was wrong. Jagr struggled to keep up with the bigger, stronger, and faster men. He finished with just eight goals and ten assists in thirty-nine games.

Despite Jagr's disappointing season, his coaches were excited about his potential. They knew their young player would eventually become a star in the league because he worked so hard. For example, Jagr stayed on the ice long after the team's practice ended and worked on his shooting and passing techniques. And at home he continued his strength-training program using his home-made weights.

Jagr was better prepared for his second professional season with Poldi Kladno. He was a more accurate shooter and passer, and he was one of the fastest players on the ice. His play improved so much that he ended the 1989–1990 season as the team's leading scorer. His outstanding season earned him a place on the Czechoslovak under-eighteen team. With this team he played in the European Championships—his first taste of international competition. During the games he impressed fans and players with his rare combination of speed and strength. The Czech team won the silver medal, and Jagr was named to the tournament all-star team.

Jagr fights to score a goal. Jagr joined the Czech pro ranks at the age of fifteen.

At age sixteen Jagr was one of the top hockey players in Europe. But he was still growing, and he had more to learn about the game. In particular, he concentrated on learning how to fake defensemen with moves instead of depending on speed alone to create scoring opportunities. His coaches and father sensed he could get even better.

One Step Away

The next season, Jagr joined the best hockey team in Czechoslovakia—the powerful men's national team. He was the youngest member on the team. In an international tournament held in Prague, he and his Czech teammates played the Calgary Flames, the best team from the NHL. Czechoslovakia won 4-1, and Jagr captured the attention of many NHL **scouts** for the first time.

Long before Jagr was born, players from Communist nations were unable to join the NHL unless they defected, or left their countries without permission. The Soviet-enforced government did not allow citizens to travel to North America. But in 1989 communism was failing in Eastern Europe and people could travel more freely. As a result, many of the best hockey players from Communist countries were moving to North America and joining the NHL.

At age seventeen Jagr was considered too young to play in the NHL, but that perception soon began to change. In 1990 he competed in the IIHF World Championships in Switzerland with the Czech men's national team. He scored three goals and two assists in the tour-

Jagr (right) blocks a New Jersey Devils player. The Czech star attracted the attention of the NHL after playing well in international competition in 1990.

nament. In the medal round he participated in the team's 3-2 victory over Canada, whose roster was filled with NHL stars. After his performance against top competition, scouts knew Jaromir Jagr was ready to play professionally in North America.

Jagr's parents were not so sure, however. They worried that their son was too young to move to a country so far from home. But Jagr's desire to play in the NHL remained strong, and there was no talking him out of it. He had worked hard to make himself a great player, and he was ready for the next step in his career.

Penguin Power

Before the 1990 NHL draft many teams were considering Jagr. The teams' scouts were impressed with his speed and puck-handling ability. But many scouts were not sure he could withstand the bruising style played in the NHL. Jagr and his fellow Europeans had learned to use speed and skill to beat defenses. But many North American players used physical contact to wear down opponents.

The Pittsburgh Penguins had scouted Jagr extensively and knew how strong he was. At six feet, two inches tall and more than two hundred pounds, he was a potential physical force on the ice. So the Penguins selected him when their turn came in the first round of the draft. On his Penguins jersey Jagr chose to wear number 68 in honor of the year in which the Prague Spring took place.

Jagr had not only made it to the top hockey league in the world—his longtime dream—he was also going to play on the same team as his idol, Mario Lemieux. He spent the summer in Kladno training for the upcoming season, then he said good-bye to his family and friends and headed for Pittsburgh, Pennsylvania, to begin his NHL career.

Jagr did not speak English, so the team's coaches and management staff did everything they could to help the eighteen-year-old feel comfortable in his new surroundings. Before **training camp** they had him take English lessons with a tutor so he could communicate with his coaches and teammates without a translator. The Penguins also arranged for him to stay with a Czech family in Pittsburgh until he was comfortable living on his own.

Rookie Blues

The team's efforts to ease Jagr into his new life in the United States did not work very well. After spending eight hours a day for two months with his tutor, he still did not understand English. And living with the Czech family did not keep him from missing his family back home.

Despite the problems Jagr had adapting to his new environment, he still seemed capable of making the Penguins better. The team needed another scorer to complement Lemieux, and the coaches hoped it would be Jagr. They were pleased with what they saw from him

Jagr joined the Pittsburgh Penguins in 1990. He chose to wear number 68 to honor the 1968 Czech revolt known as the Prague Spring.

early on. While playing **right wing** his superb skating and shooting abilities were on display in the preseason. He also answered any questions about his toughness when he withstood the hard **body checks** from opposing players.

When the 1990–1991 regular season started Jagr scored a goal in his second game, but then he began to struggle. In one fifteen-game stretch in November he did not score any goals and had only one assist. He became so frustrated during the slump that he cried after one of the games.

Because of the language barrier Jagr could not tell his coaches or teammates how he felt. He became so unhappy that he considered returning home to his family in Kladno. "It made me grow up real fast," he says about his difficult times as a rookie. "Nothing prepares you for that kind of shock."[5]

Stanley Cup Champs

The Penguins coaches sensed the language barrier and Jagr's mood were affecting his play. In an attempt to keep him from becoming even more unhappy on the team, they traded one of their players for Jiri Hrdina, Jagr's former teammate on the Czech men's team.

Hrdina immediately helped Jagr become more comfortable on the team as the two renewed their friendship. Jagr also received a boost on the ice because he was able to communicate with the coaches and players through Hrdina, who spoke English. With the two Czechs skating together, Jagr finally began to show fans what the

Penguins scouts had seen him do in Czechoslovakia. He scored thirty-seven points in the last forty games of the season. But he was just getting started.

In the 1991 play-offs Jagr led all rookies in the league in scoring by recording three goals and ten assists. He

Jagr (left) hit his stride in the 1991 play-offs leading all rookies in scoring.

even scored the overtime, series-clinching goal against the New Jersey Devils in the divisional semifinals. The Penguins went on to the Stanley Cup finals for the first time in team history.

Jagr continued to play well against the Minnesota North Stars in the finals. His five assists in the series were an NHL rookie record. They were also a big reason the Penguins beat the North Stars to win their first championship. He and his father hugged the Stanley Cup trophy in the locker room afterward. It was a dream come true for both father and son.

Mario Jr.

Jagr's second season started off much more smoothly than his first. He moved in with an American family, and his English improved. He overcame his shyness enough to give humorous weather reports on his favorite rock and roll radio station. And he became popular with female fans, who loved his good looks and long, wavy hair.

On the ice Jagr reminded people of a young Mario Lemieux. In fact, fans in Pittsburgh gave him a nickname by rearranging the letters in *Jaromir* to spell "Mario Jr." The nickname fit as Jagr continued to score goals. He and Lemieux helped the Penguins become one of the top offensive teams in the NHL. In just his second season he scored sixty-nine points and became an all-star.

Again Jagr shone brightly in the play-offs. He scored three game-winning goals. Then in Game 1 of the Stanley Cup finals against the Chicago Blackhawks, he

Jagr's (left) playing style reminded fans of a young Mario Lemieux (right). Jagr and Lemieux helped the Pittsburgh Penguins become one of the best teams in the NHL.

achieved superstar status. With the Penguins trailing by a goal late in the game, he intercepted a pass deep in the Penguins' end and raced down the ice. He faked one defenseman, slid the puck between the legs of another, and muscled his way past a third before backhanding the game-tying goal under the goaltender. The Penguins fans went wild. Lemieux then scored the winning goal with twelve seconds left. The two goals set the tone for the series as the Penguins swept the Blackhawks in four games and won their second straight Stanley Cup title.

Lemieux later called Jagr's goal in the first game of the finals "the sweetest goal I've ever seen."[6] He also told reporters the young Czech was someday going to be the greatest hockey player in the world—a title Lemieux held at the time.

CHAPTER FOUR

World's Best

During the 1992–1993 season Mario Lemieux was diagnosed with Hodgkin's disease, a form of cancer, and the team looked to Jagr to step into Lemieux's leadership role. But with the Penguins' best player out of the lineup, Jagr struggled as opposing teams no longer had to worry about stopping two stars. They had to concentrate mainly on him. In the nineteen games Lemieux missed, Jagr lost his confidence on the ice. He scored just five goals and was booed by the fans for the first time.

Part of Jagr's problem was his tendency to try to do too much on the ice. Often when he was free for a shot, he tried one more dazzling move to skate past his defender. He was usually successful, but by then he had lost the opportunity to shoot.

Despite his lack of scoring chances, Jagr finished the regular season with thirty-four goals. He also had sixty assists to finish second on the team in scoring, behind Lemieux. The Penguins finished the regular season 56-21-7, their best record ever. Lemieux returned in time for the play-offs and the Penguins beat the New Jersey Devils in the first round. In the second round against the New York Islanders, however, Lemieux struggled with an injury and Jagr went scoreless in the last two games—both losses. This ended the team's hopes for a third Stanley Cup appearance.

Pittsburgh fans criticized Jagr for not taking the team to the championship. Some of his teammates accused him of being immature. They said he sometimes lost his temper during practice and pouted if he did not score in a game. The complaints angered Jagr and made him feel unappreciated. He asked to be traded to another team. The Penguins management refused his request. They knew Jagr was still young and would learn to play better even without Lemieux.

Scoring Champion

The 1994 season did not start on time because the league's owners and players had a dispute over salaries and other money-related issues. To stay in shape while the two sides worked out their differences, Jagr returned to the Czech Republic. There he played for his old professional team, Poldi Kladno. He scored twenty-two points in just eleven games, and seemed to regain the confidence he had missed the previous season.

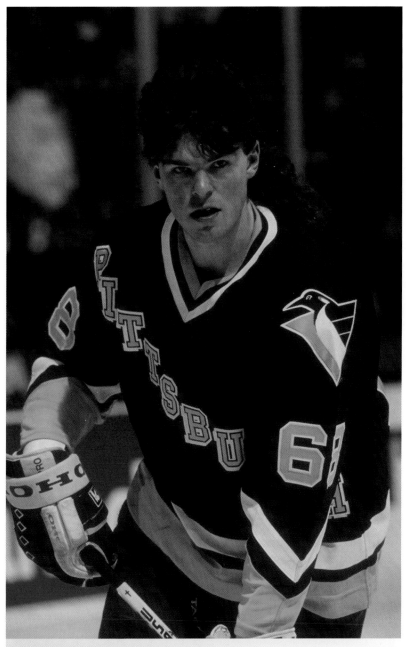

Jagr, seen here in 1993 at the age of twenty-one, was accused by his Penguin teammates during the 1992–1993 season of being immature.

Jagr's Hockey Statistics

Season	Team	Games Played	Goals	Assists	Total Points
1990–1991	Penguins	80	27	30	57
1991–1992	Penguins	70	32	37	69
1992–1993	Penguins	81	34	60	94
1993–1994	Penguins	80	32	67	99
1994–1995	Penguins	48	32	38	70
1995–1996	Penguins	82	62	87	149
1996–1997	Penguins	63	47	48	95
1997–1998	Penguins	77	35	67	102
1998–1999	Penguins	81	44	83	127
1999–2000	Penguins	63	42	54	96
2000–2001	Penguins	81	52	69	121
2001–2002	Capitals	69	31	48	79
2002–2003*	Capitals	64	34	35	69
NHL Totals		939	504	723	1227

*2002–2003 season totals through February 2003

Source: National Hockey League.

The NHL work stoppage was not the only time Jagr traveled to the Czech Republic. He also spent his summers in Kladno with his family. During his time there he often visited hospitals and played with children who had life-threatening illnesses such as cancer. He also traveled to hockey rinks in the area and gave kids skating and shooting lessons. Jagr explains why he returned home whenever he was not playing hockey. "It helps me keep a stable outlook on life. I like to play [in the Czech Republic] with the young kids because it is a special part of our tradition . . . guys who are playing in the pros now always come back to help develop the stars of the future. It's something you don't see in the United States, which is really too bad."[7]

When the NHL salary dispute ended in January 1995 Jagr was eager to continue the success he enjoyed with Poldi Kladno. Lemieux was sidelined for the entire season with a bad back, but this time Jagr filled in admirably. He scored an amazing twenty-eight points in the first thirteen games. In the forty-eighth and final game of the season he scored his seventieth point and became the first European-trained player to win the Art Ross Trophy, an award given to the NHL's top scorer.

The Penguins lost in the second round of the play-offs, but there were few complaints about Jagr's play this time. He was a definite superstar in the league and was close to making Lemieux's early prediction come true. He seemed ready to become the greatest player in the game.

Captain Jagr

Lemieux returned the next season and Jagr excelled once again. He scored 149 points, the greatest offensive output for a right wing in NHL history. He finished second in the league in scoring behind Lemieux.

That year, the Penguins won the Northeast Division title and entered the play-offs playing well. In the second round against the New York Rangers, Jagr and Lemieux both scored three goals apiece in one game, an astonishing feat. But the Penguins' season ended in the conference semifinals when the Florida Panthers held both stars well below their scoring averages.

Lemieux retired after the 1996–1997 season because of chronic back problems. Jagr was named team captain in his place. At the age of twenty-four, Jagr was the

Jagr cuts around the back of the net during a semifinals game against the Florida Panthers in May 1996. Jagr's team was defeated in the series.

team's new leader. He explained at the time how a change in attitudes made the transition possible. "I was a troublemaker [in his early years with the team]," he says. "When I wasn't happy, I would scream—I was uninterested in what I did on the ice or whatever the team did. I changed, because a lot of players look up to me now. I am trying to lead by example."[8]

A Fresh Start

Jagr kept getting better, even with Lemieux out of the game. Besides winning his second NHL scoring title during the 1997–1998 season, he led the Czech Republic past Russia (formerly the Soviet Union) for the gold medal in the 1998 Winter Olympics. It was one of the proudest moments in his life.

Jagr won the NHL's MVP award by scoring 127 points in the 1998–1999 season. Experts agreed that Jagr was the world's greatest hockey player. Still, he grew more frustrated each year when his team failed to reach the Stanley Cup finals. Even with Lemieux's surprise return in 2000, the Penguins' season ended short of a championship.

After winning his fourth straight scoring title in 2000, Jagr requested a trade. He was ready for a change. This time the Penguins honored Jagr's request and traded him to the Washington Capitals. He was sad to be leaving Pittsburgh, his home for more than ten years, but he was excited to be starting a new chapter in his career.

The 2001–2002 season did not go as well as Jagr and the Capitals had hoped. He was injured most of the

Jagr and his mother, Anna, admire the Lester B. Pearson trophy awarded to the star for being the NHL's most valuable player in 1999.

season, his scoring dropped to seventy-nine points, and Washington missed the play-offs. Despite this, many people still consider Jaromir Jagr to be one of the best players in the NHL.

At age thirty-one Jagr is in the prime of his professional career. But his life is no longer devoted entirely to playing hockey. In recent years he has dated several women, two of whom are European models and another who is a television sports reporter in the Czech Republic. He hopes to one day settle down, get married, and start a family. Jagr also places great importance on being a role model to Czech citizens, people who are still recovering from their long struggle for freedom. "Freedom is nothing to take lightly," he says. "If I don't work hard at my job, the people in Czechoslovakia might not realize the opportunities we have here. Kids in Czechoslovakia look up to me . . . and I'm never going to set a bad example for them."[9]

Notes

Chapter One: Breaking Free

1. Quoted in Larry Wigge, "Star Appeal: Pittsburgh Penguins' Jaromir Jagr," *Sporting News*, April 15, 1996, p. 56.

2. Quoted in E.M. Swift, "NHL Preview '92–93," *Sports Illustrated*, October 12, 1992, p. 40.

3. Quoted in Swift, "NHL Preview '92–93," p. 41.

4. Quoted in Lou Cannon, *President Reagan: The Role of a Lifetime.* New York: Public Affairs, 2000, p. 273.

Chapter Three: Penguin Power

5. Quoted in William Drozdiak, "The Hip Czech," *Washington Post*, June 28, 2001, p. A01.

6. Quoted in William Gildea, "Magical Jagr Can Make Penguins Take Flight," *Washington Post*, April 12, 2000, p. D01.

Chapter Four: World's Best

7. Quoted in Drozdiak, "The Hip Czech," p. A01.

8. Quoted in Chris McDonnell, *Hockey's Greatest Stars: Legends and Young Lions.* Willowdale, Ontario: Firefly Books, 1999, p. 72.

9. Quoted in Wigge, "Star Appeal," p. 56.

Glossary

all-star: A player who is voted by the fans to the All-Star game for his outstanding play.

assist: A pass to a teammate that leads to a goal.

body check: Strong physical contact used by a defender to keep an offensive player from getting to or maintaining the puck.

goal: A shot that goes between the goal posts.

right wing: A position in which a hockey player covers the right side of the ice while on offense.

scout: A person who evaluates a player's talent.

slap shot: A shot in hockey made by swinging the stick at the puck.

Stanley Cup: The trophy given to the team that wins the NHL championship; named after Lord Stanley, an Englishman appointed as Governor General of Canada in 1888.

training camp: The period of time in which a team prepares for the regular season.

For Further Exploration

Books

Michael Harling, *Hockey Heroes: Jaromir Jagr*. Vancouver/Toronto/New York: Greystone, 2001. A biography of the NHL's most exciting player. It details his earliest days on the ice as a boy in Czechoslovakia to his first season with the Washington Capitals.

Chris McDonnell, *Hockey's Greatest Stars: Legends and Young Lions*. Willowdale, Ontario: Firefly Books, 1999. Examines the top eighty NHL players of all time, including Wayne Gretzky, Gordie Howe, Jaromir Jagr, and Mario Lemieux.

Arthur Pincus, *The Official Illustrated NHL History: The Story of the Coolest Game on Earth*. Chicago: Triumph Books, 1999. Includes a detailed history of the NHL, complete with photographs, famous-player profiles, individual and team records, and more.

Dean Schabner, *Jaromir Jagr*. Philadelphia: Chelsea House, 2000. Examines Jagr's life and career—from his childhood in Czechoslovakia to his rise to fame with the Pittsburgh Penguins. Includes photos, chronology, and career statistics.

Internet Sources

CBS.SportsLine.com, "NHL-#68 Jaromir Jagr." www.cbs. sportsline.com. A great source for Jagr's career and situational statistics, game log information, and team news.

ESPN.com, "Jaromir Jagr." http://sports.espn.go.com. Provides an up-to-date resource for Jagr's statistics.

Website

Washington Capitals Official Site (www.washingtoncaps. com). Includes Washington Capitals game articles, player info, team history, multimedia, and more.

Index

Picture Credits

Cover image: © Reuters NewMedia Inc./CORBIS

© AFP/CORBIS, 29

Associated Press, AP, 19, 21, 25, 36, 38

Getty Images, 5, 11, 12, 27, 33

© Hulton-Deutsch Collection/CORBIS, 9

Chris Jouan, 8, 34

© Reuters NewMedia Inc./CORBIS, 15, 17

About the Author

Raymond H. Miller is the author of more than fifty nonfiction books for children. He has written on a range of topics from baseball card collecting to volcanoes. Miller enjoys playing sports and spending time outdoors with his wife and two daughters.